arty dogs

Written by David Baird

Illustrated by Mauriec Broughton

Stewart, Tabori & Chang
NEW YORK

contents

introduction

There is a tendency to call certain tales "shaggy dog stories"—well, in time-honored tradition the following have been harvested through the ages from some of the shaggiest dogs. In fact, it is probably fair to say that these are 100 percent genuine shaggy dog stories, each absolutely faithful to its source: rumors from neighbors; notes jotted on the backs of sketches; gossip from the dog pound; forgotten biographies; half-remembered facts, and unpublished works. The stories will show you how it is possible that dogs have influenced the art world we know and love today. The certain thing is that wherever dogs are, humor is sure to follow. These glimpses into the canine rewriting of art history will soon have you lying on your back on the kitchen floor waiting to have your tummy rubbed.

How long have dogs been influencing art? More than two thousand years, if this design is anything to go by. The study is thought to date back to the Hellenistic period circa 25 BC. It was a preliminary sketch for a sculpture from the workshop of Agesandar, Athenodoros, and Polydoros and is believed to portray the Trojan priest Laocoon and his sons. These men warned their compatriots not to accept the gigantic Trojan Horse that concealed Greek soldiers, thus foiling a devious plan for the destruction of Troy.

The grateful dogs of Troy are shown here expressing their appreciation to their saviors with licks from pink marble tongues. The public of the time, however, who took pleasure in more dramatic spectacles, such as gladiatorial fights, found the subject too timid, and the plans for the sculpture were sent back for a rethink.

A few weeks later, modified sketches were submitted, and the sculpture was finally approved. Now on display in the Vatican Museum, this second work is definitely of much less interest to dog lovers. It features two gigantic sea snakes, sent by vengeful gods, coiling around and suffocating the priest and his sons as punishment for thwarting their plan to destroy Troy.

But the story doesn't end here. Legend has it that the sculpture was secretly finished, according to the original plans, and that the gods who favored Troy brought the pack of marble dogs to life. The happy hounds were then sent off to roam the countryside and to attack any enemies of Troy with their pink tongues.

The Florentine artist Alesso Baldovinetti was a bit of a rogue, or so the story goes. Not only was he a ladies' man, he also enjoyed the occasional bet on dog races. After much persuading, his local priest managed to swear him off both pursuits, but passion and risk were so close to the artist's heart that it was not long before he was up to his old tricks again.

The artist is believed to have fallen in love with a married woman of great beauty whose portrait he began painting one balmy summer evening. Things were just getting romantic when the priest arrived, unannounced. Baldovinetti's model had just enough time to hide behind a screen, but the artist's canvas—which revealed the outline of a woman's yellow dress with palm leaf motif—was left in full view.

"Ah," exclaimed the priest, "I can see that you are still a womanizer! Where have you hidden her?" As he stooped to search beneath the bed, the artist replied, "Father, I assure you I was not painting a woman, but a dog. You made me stop betting, but said nothing of capturing the beauty of the canine form in paint!"

The priest viewed the canvas with suspicion. "And who has ever seen a dog dressed in such attire?"

The artist weighed his response carefully before replying, "Those are racing colors—all will become clear if you allow me to finish the picture." Under the priest's watchful gaze, Baldovinetti completed the painting, shown here, of a racing hound named Lady, whose number was 9 and who won the local championship that year at odds of 8-1. The priest was satisfied and removed himself from the studio, allowing the artist to pursue his other passion.

This picture is thought to have provoked a legal investigation into the activities of the artist Giuseppe Arcimboldo in Milan during the summer of 1573. It was a particularly glorious summer, and there was an abundance of fresh fruit and vegetables to be harvested. The renowned artist was invited to celebrate God's bountiful gifts in a series of paintings composed of the foods of the region.

In order to do this, Arcimboldo constructed two life-size models of dogs out of marzipan. His plan was to decorate them with fruits and vegetables and then paint them on canvas. What he hadn't planned for was the interference of his nosy neighbor, a widow by the name of Señora Bumbolini.

Leaning over her balcony to see what the artist was up to, she caught a glimpse of something that horrified her. From her slightly obscured vantage point, she could just make out Arcimboldo, and he appeared to be sticking long spikes with cucumbers, flowers, grapes, and leaves attached, into what appeared to be two little dogs.

Things came to a head when the artist completed the picture, and local children were allowed to eat the models. The poor woman nearly died of shock and called for the police who, to her amazement, joined the feast.

Michelangelo da Cravaggio is one of those artists who had the capacity to astonish his public. It is said that in his work can be seen the beginnings of modern art. His models were recruited from the ranks of coarse peasants, Roman youths, and ladies of the night. He was regularly in trouble with authority and on one occasion is said to have procured the body of drowned prostitute to use as the model for the Virgin.

Apparently he was arrested and locked in jail for the night. The arresting officer had a rather butch dog named Barkus who sat outside the artist's cell all night, growling at every move he made, barking each time he nodded off. When the artist did eventually manage to sleep, he was awakened rather abruptly by the brute canine urinating on his head. Caravaggio swore his revenge.

On his release, the artist painted this portrait of the beast, which he called *The Young Barkus,* and exhibited it next door to the prison. At the sight of the painting, the locals were reduced to fits of laughter, the terror hound's status to one of "big softy." The officer who owned Barkus became the laughing stock of the area and resigned. The avenged artist went on to use the same composition for another painting in which he replaced the dog Barkus with a young Roman boy wearing vine leaves. Titled *The Young Bacchus,* this painting became one of the most famous that Caravaggio ever painted.

$\mathcal{S}$ir Anthony Van Dyck entered Peter Paul Rubens's studio around 1618 as an assistant. He was quick to learn the master's techniques but always managed to retain his own style. There is a very well-known self-portrait of the artist clutching a large sunflower, but what is not so well-known is that it was all the result of a misunderstanding.

Van Dyck had a rather handsome lurcher dog, which he named Sunflower because he was tall and stately. This faithful hound would sit outside the studio patiently as his master painted. One day Rubens, who was growing deaf, heard Van Dyck say that he was going to take some water to Sunflower who was thirsty. Rubens misheard completely and thought the young artist was going to water some flowers. Keen to foster the love of nature in his young protégé, Rubens suggested that Van Dyck paint a self-portrait with a sunflower. Excited by the idea, the young artist set about the challenge with enthusiasm.

Several days later Van Dyck invited Rubens to view the finished work. On seeing the painting of his assistant tickling the chest of a dog, Rubens knocked a jug containing brushes to the ground in anger and exclaimed: "Is this some kind of prank? I instructed you to paint a self-portrait with a sunflower, not a mangy mutt! Now go and pick some flowers and start again!"

Understanding his master's mistake and not wishing to anger him further, Van Dyck obliged. The resulting painting has enjoyed much critical acclaim, unlike the earlier version, which, despite its canine charm, languished in Sunflower's kennel.

Anyone who has delved into the famous story of *The Three Musketeers* by Alexandre Dumas will have no difficulty in recognizing the imposing figure of Cardinal Richelieu shown here. The Brussels-born artist Philippe de Champaigne saw fit to pose the cardinal like some erupting volcano complete with the fiery flow of lava suggested by the scarlet robes.

It is thought that this curious version of Champaigne's masterpiece surfaced recently among the goods and chattels of Dumas. It features a dog determinedly attempting to seize in its jowls the crimson biretta that Richelieu holds in his outstretched hand. Lengthy research has thrown some light upon the origin of this curiosity.

It seems that Dumas may originally have intended the heroes of his story to be canine. At one time, it is believed, Dumas owned several dogs from a single litter, one of which he called d'Artagnan. In one of his notebooks he makes copious references to these "dogs with ears like muskets." Apparently Dumas's publisher persuaded the reluctant author to change the title of his novel from *The Three Musket-Ears* to *The Three Musketeers*.

The world of canine literature is doubtless poorer for this change, and Dumas is believed to have been upset by his surrender to commercial considerations. It is thought that he commissioned this painting of his beloved d'Artagnan with Cardinal Richelieu as a personal reminder of what *should* have been. If he couldn't immortalize his pets in his literature then he would immortalize them in paint.

*J*an Vermeer was among the finest Dutch painters of the seventeenth century. His peaceful, poetic compositions possess a wonderful calmness for today's viewer.

This charming little picture has a rather romantic canine tale attached to it. It is thought that the woman featured in this picture was called Henrika, and that the terrier in the portrait on the wall was a good-natured local stray named Cupid.

Depressed after the death of her beloved dog Toodles, Henrika had become morose. She closed her curtains to shut out the world and locked up her virginal—solitude and silence now replaced the musical moments she and Toodles had shared.

Cupid, as though sensing her grief, arrived at her door one fine spring evening. There he stood, wagging his tail and barking eagerly. Henrika felt certain that he was trying to draw her attention to something important and joined him outside where, from behind a wall emerged a fine, white-coated dog. Henrika shrieked, turned pale, staggered backward, and collapsed on the floor. Anyone would think she had seen a ghost!

The mysterious white dog was the mirror image of her dear departed Toodles. Chance had brought this poor, friendless pooch to her doorstep. Cupid's magic worked instantly—Henrika adopted her departed pet's "twin" without hesitation. The curtains were opened, the virginal was unlocked, and a beautiful friendship began. Cupid, meanwhile, strolled off into the sunset. This composition was commissioned by way of thanks for the part he played in bringing two lonely hearts together.

Pietro Longhi's paintings, though interesting, never really helped him to achieve the greatness of other Venetian artists. But with his almost scientific curiosity, he *did* capture many events that inform us of the time.

Take the recreational pastimes of the "upper crust" in Venice for example. Many wondered how Venetians managed to get themselves worked up to such a frenzy prior to celebrating Carnival. These *Cangiarsi* fascinated Longhi. He approached them and asked if he could tag along on one of their pre-Carnival outings and capture their enjoyment on canvas. He was made to feel welcome and was quite taken back to discover that their source of entertainment was nothing other than a dog show—probably the first of its kind.

Longhi swiftly began painting—recording for posterity the reveler's reaction to seeing the first public appearance of a pair of shar-pei dogs. Never before had Europe seen such animals. The artist painted furiously as the group's enthusiasm became uncontainable and the air filled with outbursts of ecstasy: "*Ohi la! Eccomi!…avendo veduta a volo d'uccello!*" ("Hey man! Look at me…I've got a bird's-eye view!")

Quite exhausted by the experience, the artist asked their leader, "Is it always like this?" to which the man replied: "Not always. Why don't you come along next Carnival when we shall have a rhinoceros."

Painted by Thomas Gainsborough to celebrate the marriage of Robert Andrews and Frances Carter in 1748, this famous work of art shows the happy couple at rest following a morning's shoot in the English countryside. But did you know that the version of this painting on display at the National Gallery in London is believed to be incomplete? On *that* canvas Mrs. Andrew's dress is unfinished and there is, to the trained eye, the outline of a bird visible on her lap—suggesting that a pheasant was to have been included in the composition.

Rumor has it that the painting was an earlier version of the one shown here. Apparently on their wedding day, Mr. and Mrs. Andrews combined their households of hunting dogs, causing much excitement among the animals. It is thought that just as Gainsborough was putting the finishing touches on his painting, the unruly bunch of dogs came racing across the field, snatched the pheasant from Mrs. Andrews's lap, and ran off with it. Mr. Andrews pursued the pack and scolded them for their bad manners. This painting was then produced with the troublemakers leaning against their mistress in obsequious apology, while the smallest of the pack sits angelically on her lap.

$\mathcal{S}$ir Henry Raeburn was one of Scotland's most popular artists in the early nineteenth century. He painted as many as one thousand portraits of Edinburgh poets and dignitaries, scholars, lairds, philosophers, and clergy. His work, complete with all its humor, so pleased King George IV that he made him a knight.

One of Raeburn's best-loved portraits is *The Reverend Robert Walker Skating on Duddingston Loch*, in which a theatrically posed, black-clad minister is shown skating against a wintry background. But did you know that we have a rather worried dog to thank for the famous image?

Every Sunday, the reverend would make the difficult journey to present his sermon in the three churches to which he ministered. On winter mornings, he was seen regularly slipping and sliding across the frozen loch, dragging behind him his fox terrier Whiskey. He would invariably end up carrying the dog in his arms, making him late for the service. One morning, however, a member of his congregation suggested loudly in a thick Scots brogue: "Why dinna ye git yer skates on laddie an' whilst yer at it, put some on yer wee doggie, too!"

Well, no sooner said than done. The next week, the reverend dusted off the skates he'd used as a young man and adapted an old snow ski to accommodate his dog. From that day on, the two could be seen crossing the frozen waters of Duddingston Loch every winter Sunday, and the sermons were never delivered late again. It is thought that this is how Raeburn's portrait of Reverend Robert Walker looked originally before removing the dog "to preserve the dignity of the church."

William Blake was a man of great depth, a visionary, poet, prophet, and symbolist. He is best remembered for his famous hymn *Jerusalem*, which was almost adopted as England's national anthem.

Among Blake's other works is an engraving titled *The Ancient of Days*, in which a godlike being reaches down from the heavens bearing a pair of compasses. But what on earth is he measuring?

Scholars and art historians around the world have pondered this question for years, but it was a French professor, Monsieur Neuf, who came closest to explaining the phenomenon. This learned gentleman took as his starting place the immortal first line of *Jerusalem*: "And did those feet in ancient time walk upon England's pastures green…"

He noticed that in an early manuscript the words "feet" and "green" were obliterating other words that had been hastily scratched out. With the aid of a powerful magnifying glass he managed to decipher the missing word as "paws" and "chilly".

It is well-known that Blake was a great dog lover who spent many hours romping on Hampstead Heath with his faithful dachshund Rosco, but it is not so well-known that the artist was also something of a hypochondriac, who worried that his pet would catch a cold scampering about in the inclement English weather. Monsieur Neuf put two and two together and decided that if Rosco's feet on Hampstead Heath were indeed those "paws" on "England's pastures chilly," then it was more than likely that those massive compasses were being used to trace the exaggerated proportions of a dachshund, ready for the fitting of a snug new coat. The eccentric professor's suspicions were confirmed when the original engraving was X-rayed to reveal the scene shown here.

George Caleb Bingham was one of the most important American artists of the nineteenth century. This story concerns a newly discovered version of his famous painting *Fur Traders Descending the Missouri*, in which two figures in a laden boat glide peacefully through the morning mist.

Everyone along the river knew the two trappers and would call greetings as they passed. But one particular morning the atmosphere was strangely cold, and instead of the usually friendly encounters along the riverbank, people shouted, spat, and even threw stones.

The reason for this hostile reception was soon revealed. Arriving at the trading post, the duo were met by a group of outraged settlers who had mistaken the trader's snoozing pets for the pelts of dogs and cats.

It didn't take long for the traders to explain: "We've given up trapping. We're breeding animals now. And we've come here with these cats and dogs to open a pet shop."

The settlers were delighted, as was Bingham, who had been observing the scene. Rumor has it that he was one of the traders' first customers and was so thrilled with his new canine companion that he painted this canvas as a tribute to the enterprising trappers.

This is the "true" story behind the famous painting *Arrangement in Grey and Black, No. 1: The Artist's Mother* by James Abbott McNeill Whistler. Apparently, Whistler's Mom loved to pass time playing with Sparky, the family dalmatian. She would sit in her favorite chair, throw a ball along the hallway, and Sparky would tear off after it. Each time he returned, she would fix her gaze on a paw mark on the wall and sit motionless, like a figure in a wax museum, for two or three minutes, often longer, while the dog tried and tried to get her attention. Then, just when Sparky seemed disinterested, she would snap out of her trance, grab the ball, and hurl it once again down the hall, and everyone in the house would laugh.

When her son painted this picture to capture the event, she asked him to paint another, leaving Sparky out of it...in that way she could always remember him tearing off after the ball. An odd tale perhaps, but it does explain the expression on Mrs. Whistler's face.

No, this is *not* a scene from a hippie boating festival during the 1960s. In fact it dates back to early 1888, and though relatively unknown, it is almost certain that the world-famous painting *The Lady of Shallot* would never have existed if it were not for this earlier work.

John William Waterhouse, a follower of the Pre-Raphaelites with an interest in mythology and poetry, was enjoying a picnic by a lake. He was lying back, pondering the translation of Tennyson's beautiful lyrical poem *The Lady of Shallot* into paint, when he was woken from his reverie by a frantic commotion. A spaniel had chased some ducks into the lake and had become entangled in the rushes. Alerted by her pet's panic-stricken yelps, a young woman rowed her boat out onto the water in a valiant rescue attempt.

Inspired by the drama and pathos of the scene, the artist quickly completed this sketch. It wasn't until he returned home in the evening that he realized this was the image he had been looking for—minus the dog, of course.

This painting has less to do with dogs inspiring art than it does with dogs influencing hairstyles.

The poodle featured here was named Doggie X and was owned by Madame X, a pale woman with a long nose, who wore dark velvet clothing with gold trimmings. During the early 1920s, she is thought to have been married to a high school sports coach. The couple lived part of the year in America and the other part in London, where they encountered the Italian-born, American-raised artist John Singer Sargent.

Commissioned to paint Madame X's beloved poodle, Sargent is believed to have employed the services of a leading hairdresser to groom the dog in preparation for its sitting.

The dog's owners were delighted with the painting. When Mister X saw the hairdo on the dog, he immediately got the idea for the pom-poms, which are used by high school cheerleaders.

Meanwhile, Madame X loved the picture so much that she commissioned Sargent to paint her portrait and insisted that he use the same hairstylist. The resulting painting can be seen at the Metropolitan Museum of Art in New York City. As for Doggie X, well, for a few weeks he was the laughing stock among his canine friends, but eventually the bouffant look caught on and can be seen sported by show poodles all around the world.

The remarkable English artist Joseph Mallord William Turner was fascinated by light, air, water, and atmospheric conditions. He so enjoyed painting the conflict of the elements that he is said to have gone to such extremes as tying himself to the bow of a ship in order to capture the chaos of a storm at sea.

Once, he trudged off up into the Alps in search of snow. Wearing only the flimsiest of clothing and the determination of an artist, Turner set off into the worst weather the region had seen for seasons. When it grew dark and the artist failed to return, concerned locals sent out a rescue party in the form of a Bernese mountain dog with a flask of brandy slung securely under his neck.

Meanwhile, high in the mountains, Turner worked wildly to capture the storm that raged around him. Absorbed by his work, only when he had completed his painting did he realize the danger he was in. If it hadn't been for the bravery of the dog who soon located him, the artist would surely have frozen to death. Warmed by the brandy and reassured by his canine guide, Turner was soon delivered to safety. So grateful was he to be safe that he took the painting that had nearly cost him his life and added to it a portrait of his savior.

The painting shown here is a little-known but significant forerunner to Édouard Manet's *Un Bar Aux Folies-Bergère*. Like its more famous counterpart, this painting features the stillness of a young woman set against a background of faces, light, and movement. However *this* version helps explain why only one face is picked out in detail.

Manet regularly took his beloved French bulldog Harry to his studio, and although usually well-behaved, the poor dog acted peculiarly on this occasion. A mirror at the bar caused the chaos. All those faces looking out at him and the confusion of who was who and which was the front and back of which person…and where on earth was Harry in it all? Determined to find himself in the looking glass, Harry would pull at his leash, stand on his hind legs at the bar, and stare at his reflection. The sight was so comical that the entire ensemble fell about laughing. This was very inconvenient for the artist, who was trying to concentrate. In an attempt to restore order he issued the following ultimatum: "Ignore zee dog or else Ah weel 'av to pent only 'eem."

As Harry continued to inspect his reflection, the models found it impossible to contain their hilarity—and Manet reluctantly dismissed them. Only the young woman behind the bar was able to maintain a dignified expression—aided, it is thought, by sucking on a piece of lemon from one of the drinks she was serving. It seems that Harry was such a distraction he was banished from further compositions—what a loss to the world of art.

There was nothing that the French Impressionist painter Edgar Degas enjoyed more than providing audiences with a behind-the-scenes glimpse of theater life.

Here is a particularly heart-warming cameo of backstage life. It was Rusty the performing dog's birthday, and as a wonderful surprise, his owner, the theater manager (seen in the painting with the beard and the cane) had baked a huge birthday cake in the shape of his pet's favorite armchair. As a special treat he had also procured the services of one of the showgirls who, on a given signal, was to jump out of the cake and spin like a ballerina in a tutu covered in peppermint-flavored icing.

Unfortunately things didn't go exactly as planned, Rusty's master had underestimated the "firming" character of the icing on the tutu and mid-twirl, the dancer's costume set solid. Unable to move, a neighbor was called in to help scrape it off her. In spite of the slight hiccup it was a wonderful event for the happy dog (as you can see by his expression), and Degas liked the composition so much that he went on to complete another version of it without Rusty.

George the dalmatian was bit of a joker. One day he bet the other strays that he knew a dog who could do a perfect impersonation of a hedgehog.

"You can have my bone if he can," said the cocker spaniel.

"And my squeaky cat," added the labrador. Other such wagers were struck, and the little band of dogs followed George to a spot on the lake where a small terrier was splashing around happily. The pack assembled themselves along the bank. George gave a signal and the terrier leaped out of the water and shook himself wildly. This had two effects: the first was to send the water from his fur cascading over the audience, and the second was to make his coat stand out in a series of punkish points until he looked exactly like a hedgehog.

Unbeknownst to the happy band of dogs, the artist Paul Cézanne was seated a little further along the bank, hidden in the willows, fishing quietly for trout and inspiration. Something about the way the dogs were seated reminded him of figures by Signorelli and Michelangelo, and he hurried home and completed this sketch. Standing back from his work, he realized that something was not quite right, and sadly for the dog world (although not for George, who won his bet that day) the canine bathers were replaced by the human *Bathers* with whom we are more familiar today.

Between 1899 and 1900, Claude Monet painted many views of the Japanese-style bridge over the lily pond in his garden at Giverny. But few art lovers will have seen this one, which is believed by some to be the first in the series.

Curiously, it seems that none of the other paintings would have existed had it not been for a lonely—and somewhat confused—Alsatian who had wandered all the way from Alsace is search of his long-lost brother. Mistaking his own reflection in the lily pond for his relation, the poor animal threw himself into the water. Monet, who was wandering in his garden and saw the whole event, fished the dog from the water and dried him off. He felt so sorry for the bedraggled creature that he adopted him, and the two became inseparable.

As a tribute to his pet and to commemorate their meeting, Monet painted the picture shown here. It made quite a splash with the art world, where all were captivated by the beauty of the garden, bridge, pond, and the execution of the brushwork. But hardly anyone mentioned the dog.

This led Monet to concentrate on views "without dogs," which won him great acclaim. As for his own personal taste? If you were to have asked the artist which version of the lily pond he preferred, I suspect he would have told you the canvas with that old animal magic.

It's little surprise that Berthe Morisot found her niche as an artist. After all, she was Jean-Honoré Fragonard's granddaughter and was taught by her brother-in-law Édouard Manet.

The picture here is believed to have been a preliminary sketch of her famous work *The Cradle*. The woman shown staring tenderly at the puppies is the artist's sister and, although we can't see her full profile, it is just possible that she was pregnant at the time. The project was a lesson in time management. The goal: to create a tender scenario of a devoted mother watching over her sleeping baby. But the baby had not yet been born. In order to create the necessary maternal ambience for the composition, Morisot substituted these adorable puppies for a baby in the cradle. The effect was instant and won the desired dreamy look from her sister.

The pre-planning seems to have paid off. Morisot was able to concentrate her artistic talents solely on capturing the mood of her sister and the setting. When the baby finally arrived, all she had to do was quickly paint in its sleeping figure on top of the puppies and—*voila*—the painting was ready well in time for the christening. This version of the original painting has mysteriously survived, suggesting that although she was a devoted aunt, Morisot always had a soft spot for a cute puppy.

Pierre Auguste Renoir's painting *The Umbrellas* has had experts confused throughout history. Some believe it was painted over a period of several years; that the woman on the left and the woman on the right are wearing outfits from different periods, and that the background and even the umbrellas were added at later dates.

In the more familiar version, the woman in the foreground carries a basket and the little girl on the right is looking down at an even smaller girl holding a wooden hoop. Well, we've taken the matters into our own hands, and with the use of a pair of X-ray glasses, quite a different scene has been revealed.

The story goes something like this: Renoir, it seems, set out intending to capture a sunny day in the park. He took as his central theme a fashionable young woman walking her Irish setter named Baudelaire. Just as the artist was making some progress, it began to rain. He'd get a layer of paint down and then people would start putting on coats, many of which were still old fashioned. Then Baudelaire got wet and had to be dried. Meanwhile, umbrellas went up all over the place, and somehow a little girl appeared just as the dog's owner was collecting her basket to leave. The story is that Renoir gave up in frustration, and painted the new scene as it unfolded before him. But if the paint is scraped away, you'll find Baudelaire, still thoroughly enjoying a bracing walk through the park.

Gertrude, the Great Dane was truly psychic. But the curious thing is that her mystical powers only became apparent after the arrival of this strange old chair that her owner the Impressionist artist Paul Gauguin acquired on a trip to Java.

From the moment the chair arrived in the artist's house, Gertrude was transfixed by it. She would sit beside it for hours on end, as if conscious of an invisible presence. For Gauguin, his pet's obsession quickly became intolerable—Gertrude stopped eating, she slept only fitfully, and lost all interest in her daily walks. Even her favorite toy monkey no longer held any attraction for her. Gauguin could think of nothing else to do but make Gertrude and her chair the subject of a painting. He hoped that by capturing the scene on canvas he might understand a little better how to solve the problem. Here's the painting he did—but it changed nothing.

At his wit's end, Gauguin decided to do some research into the history of the chair itself. He discovered that it had once belonged to a young Javanese woman by the name of Annah. In the manner of a police artist, he managed to piece together a sketch of this woman from assorted descriptions gleaned from people who had known her. From this sketch, he painted another picture—this time with Annah seated in the chair. And from the moment that he completed this picture and hung it on the wall of his studio, Gertrude left the chair. Instead, she would seat herself for short periods each day in front of the portrait of *Annah the Javanese*. Nobody ever knew if Annah's ghost was really present and seated in the chair, but every now and then Gertrude would run up to the thing, sniff it, and let out a friendly bark.

Ever wondered what inspired Vincent van Gogh to paint sunflowers? Take a look at the picture here and all will become clear. The story goes that one hot day while the artist was busy painting with his studio door open, this mutt walked in and introduced himself by dropping a ball at the artist's feet. Sensing that the dog wanted to play, van Gogh hurled the ball into the street below and returned to preparing his canvas. A few minutes later, the dog was back, and this time he carried a stick in his mouth. He dropped this at van Gogh's feet. The artist picked it up, and giving the pooch a pat on the head, asked:

"And what will you turn up with next? A flower perhaps?" With that he threw the stick through the window and off ran the dog. Several more minutes passed and then the same dog came strolling through the door and, pleased with himself, placed a great big sunflower at van Gogh's feet.

"You are one clever dog, my friend. How would you like me to paint your picture?" asked the artist. The uncanny canine barked enthusiastically, took the flower in his teeth and sat with this expression from the moment van Gogh began until he completed his final brushstroke.

"What do you think?" asked the artist and the dog came to look at his portrait. He dropped the sunflower to the floor, wagged his tail, raised himself onto his hind legs, licked van Gogh's face, and then disappeared, never to be seen again. All that remained was the sunflower, the memory of a happy moment shared—and of course, the inspiration for a whole new series of paintings.

You may have seen pictures by the pointillistic artist Georges Seurat before, but probably never this one, which is really not surprising.

This particular painting shows a number of dogs lounging on the riverbank where they would gather daily to hear Marcel, a local harmonica player, belting out doggie favorites while half-submerged in the cooling waters of the Seine. (Can you spot which one is enjoying a specially requested rendition of *Ow Much Ees Zat Doggie in Zee Window?*)

Marcel, a keen entrepreneur, quickly realized that he could turn a few quick extra francs each week by providing a much needed dog-sitting service for the workers who toiled in the distant factories in the background of this picture.

So successful was his business, and indeed his musical career, that he soon had enough money to commission another painting from Seurat. This one featured his paying patrons, similarly at riverside rest, relaxing to Marcel's melodies. That painting is thought to be the famous *Bathers at Asnières,* which today hangs at the National Gallery in London.

No artist did more to capture the atmosphere of late nineteenth-century Paris than Henri de Toulouse-Lautrec. Many of his best-known works feature the activities at the Moulin Rouge—a popular nightspot for visitors to Paris and *the* haunt for the artistic community. Famous for its wild and raucous women, many a gentleman found himself tempted to taste forbidden fruits under its roof. And when the music was loud and the feathers and frills fluttered flirtatiously, it was hard to remain uninvolved.

Toulouse-Lautrec featured one such fellow in a painting titled *At the Moulin Rouge 1892*. A dapper gentleman, named Mr. Warner, is pictured chatting with two colorful-looking ladies and is consequently often referred to as "The Flirt." But Mr. Warner wasn't the only flirt around, as has become clear with the discovery of the painting shown here. Apparently this spunky Airedale turned up regularly at the venue to seek the attention of the showgirls, who pampered him. He, too, became known as "The Flirt," but whenever the amorous Englishman was out of town, the girls affectionately referred to the dog as Mr. Warner. When it came to seeking attention, there was very little to tell them apart. Some even believed the dog and the Englishman were one and the same as, curiously, they were never at the Moulin Rouge at the same time.

Friday night was bath night in the household of Pierre Bonnard—for everyone, including the dog. And, being an artist's household, it was quite usual for passersby to catch glimpses of people coming from or going to the bathtub in various degrees of undress. Everyone, that was, apart from Sophie, the artist's dog, who it seems was incredibly shy. It was absurd really. The dog would prance around all week secure in her mottled coat of golden fur, but the moment that people around her began undressing, she would slink away and grab her personal towel. Holding it with her teeth, she would swing her head from side to side and flick the towel over her back. And there she would stay until everyone else had put *their* clothes back on.

Some believe that the only reason Bonnard began to paint nudes was to get Sophie used to seeing naked people. It is not known if his scheme worked, and as this is the only painting of Sophie either dressed or undressed we will probably never know if the bashful dog ever came to terms either with her own nudity, or that of those around her.

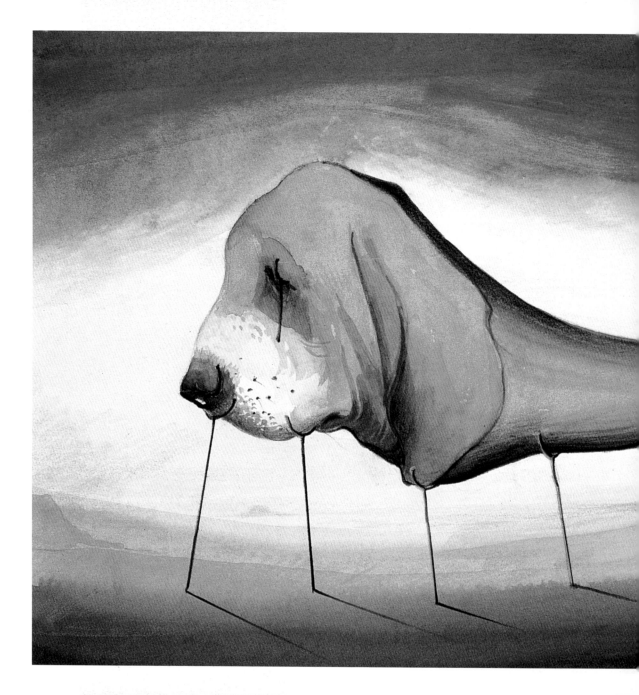

The French artist Henri Rousseau had a fondness for exotic subjects, as can be seen in this painting, *Tiger in a Tropical Storm (Surprised!).*

But where did the inspiration for this stunning painting come from? Paris is hardly associated with jungles, that is, unless you are familiar with *Les Jardin des Plantes*—a botanical garden off the tourist path with a small zoo and natural history museum. Rousseau was there one day working on a study of rubber plants, Swiss cheese plants, and the like. As usual he was accompanied by his dog Voltaire, a handsome English pointer. While the artist was working, his dog wandered freely around the park. But when the time came to go home, Voltaire was nowhere to be found. Rousseau's search led him to the little zoo where he discovered his pet, absolutely rigid next to the cage that was exhibiting a somewhat startled looking tiger.

With his tail erect, ears pricked, and foreleg raised, Voltaire did as his nature dictated and stood in a fixed stance, pointing at the tiger. Well, for an artist it was a gift. Two absolutely still, living models. Rousseau swiftly added the animals to the exotic plants he already had down on canvas and, *voila—Tiger in a Tropical Storm (Surprised!).*

The passion and intense energy in the paintings of Edvard Munch led to him being widely acclaimed as the founder of Expressionism. And just look at the expression of this poor fellow. The title —*Jealousy*—speaks volumes....

After many years Munch become convinced that he was the human alter ego of a dog that belonged to his young mistress, Eva. The artist and his lover spent many happy afternoons together, strolling through the young woman's orchard. Often Eva would reach up and pick a small crab apple from a tree and hurl it across the grass for her faithful old dog to fetch. The trusty hound would enthusiastically retrieve it, bound back to his mistress and lick her face.

But then Eva met a new lover. This handsome gentleman presented her with a lively young puppy as a token of his undying affection. Needless to say, the fickle young madam forgot all about her faithful old hound—and her old lover. This painting is a particularly touching portrayal of the old artist's anguish, as he saw his position usurped by a younger pretender.

This work of art is thought to be by the French painter Henri Matisse. It looks like three greyhounds taking a break from racing to concentrate upon a game of catch.

Rumor has it that Matisse adopted a retired racing greyhound which, even in its old age, was so fast and nimble that when it played with a ball, it gave the impression of being three dogs, not just one. This optical illusion was the inspiration for an experiment in expression and color that flaunted the rules of convention.

According to the artist, this apparently simple picture is the source of an incredible visual experience. If you hold the picture with the ball against the tip of your nose, spin it around several times (counterclockwise) and then quickly transfer your gaze to a blank piece of paper, you will see the spinning image, the dogs barking, and then it will become a single greyhound. It's not the same for everyone, of course. Perfecting it may take time. Try it, but don't get a blister on your nose.

Born in Holland in 1872, Piet Mondrian was a leading figure of modern art. But did he actually set out to do that? Evidence recently revealed suggests that he may have had quite a different ambition.

Mondrian studied art in Amsterdam and began his career painting landscapes. He then spent some time in Paris where he was heavily influenced by the Cubists and returned home filled with new ideas. Shortly after he arrived back in Amsterdam, he was approached to design an innovative new project in the center of the city: a dog sanctuary. He set about the commission with relish, incorporating all that he had learned in Paris. The central design concept was every enclosure that was to hold a homeless dog would relate to its occupant by blocks of color coordinated with the animal's fur.

Sadly for the world of architecture, Mondrian was forced to abandon the project with the outbreak of World War II. Moving first to England and then to America, he was determined not to waste all his years of planning. It was in New York, amid a growing trend for abstract and Cubist art, that he finally had the brainstorm to recycle his work. He simply erased the dogs from the preliminary sketches for his sanctuary, leaving only the cages with their strong vertical and horizontal lines and blocks of primary color. With this fresh new work he won the admiration of the nation instantly. But he never forgot where his success came from. It is told that he regularly procured marrow bones from the butcher to give to any deserving strays he encountered.

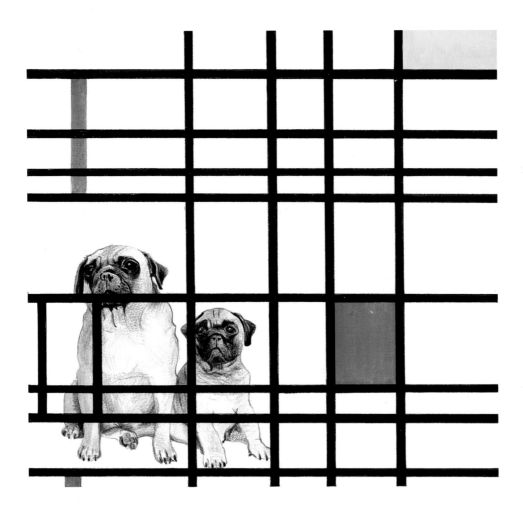

$\mathcal{W}$assily Kandinsky was a pioneer of abstract painting who founded the Russian Academy. This painting, though, is a curiosity, and until recently, no one knew it existed. It is actually one of a series of three, of which only one is known to the general public.

Kandinsky, it seems, painted the first in this mysterious series after being inspired by a couple of kittens that one of his neighbors had recently acquired. He had been considering breaking away from purely abstract subject matter for awhile, and the two cute little frolicking bundles of fluff provided him with the perfect change to his hard-edged geometrical style. Once the painting was completed, Kandinsky hung it on the wall and stepped back to admire his work. What he hadn't allowed for though was the incredible jealousy of his dog, Oscar.

Oscar had never had so much as a cartoon drawn of him, and the sight of the two cats on his master's work sent him into a jealous rage. He flew at the painting in an attempt to catch and remove the cats. Kandinsky, feeling a little guilty at having overlooked his pet's feelings, swiftly completed a second version of the painting, featuring a very red and angry Oscar. His demanding pet was still not happy, and having to share a canvas with those infuriating cats made him angrier. Totally exasperated by the whole situation, Kandinsky set to work on the third and final canvas in this series. A complete return to the pure abstract, and in a desperate plea for domestic harmony, it featured neither cats nor dogs.

It is a little-known fact that Pablo Picasso adored dogs and couldn't bear to be without one. His particular favorite was a cheeky mongrel hound whom he called Frika.

Like all dogs, Frika was very good at begging for tidbits. She could often be found in the kitchen begging for odd scraps and goodies from Picasso's rather highly strung cook, Clara. And of all tasty morsels Frika's favorite was sausages.

One day Picasso was planning a cocktail party, and Clara was diligently preparing a range of savory nibbles to be served to the guests. There was no disguising that one of the dishes contained cocktail sausages, and Frika's tastebuds were aroused. When the coast was clear, the crafty dog crept into the kitchen and spotted a small bag perched on the edge of the table. Convinced that it contained the sausages, Frika swallowed down the contents in one gulp. The poor dog had no idea that these little sausage-shaped objects were in fact red-hot chili peppers. She grimaced and howled, rolled on the floor, and pawed at her tongue. And then the cook came into the kitchen. On seeing Frika with her whole face aflame, Clara opened her mouth wide and let out the most hideous, blood-curdling scream.

Hearing the commotion, Picasso came running, but fortunately he saw the funny side of the situation. Some art historians even consider the event to have been a stylistic turning point. Picasso painted the little-known work shown here as a stern warning to Frika, who, incidentally, never touched another sausage.

It began on a Saturday night in one of those all-night cafés that Edward Hopper is said to have visited occasionally for inspiration. There was something about the lighting and the people in those places that helped him achieve a haunting feeling of isolation. And, if you looked hard enough, there was always a story.

Take the subject of this picture, for instance. Hopper stumbled onto this man sitting at the counter staring into his coffee, looking forlorn.

"Hey. What's up pal?" the artist asked.
Without looking up from the rim of his cup, the sad fellow, said slowly through a slightly trembling lip, "Buster's...gone!"

Curiously, the artist interrogated the waitress further.

"He's been like that for hours. I keep pouring out the cold coffee and refilling his cup, but he just stares into it," she said. "Says his dog's missing."

Intrigued by the tale, Hopper decided to stick around. Toward midnight, he followed the guy into the street where, like some tragic player, he'd stop for a moment and, in a low voice call "Buster," but no dog came. Saturday night became Sunday morning and, exhausted from searching, he slumped on the sidewalk in despair. The artist, feeling the subject for a new painting coming on, began sketching from the opposite side of the street. Then, from nowhere Buster suddenly appeared.

What a great story. I got it from a waitress, and it seems to hold water even if Buster here doesn't!

There is a painting by Russian-born artist Marc Chagall called *Above the Town*—in which a man and woman float across the sky. Wrapped in each other's arms, they hover above a fairy-tale landscape. But what on earth could inspire such a magical painting?

Chagall, like so many artists, had a weakness for dogs and would sit for hours at the window watching his neighbor's borzoi hounds racing around the garden.

One morning, lacking of inspiration, Chagall was strolling beside the extremely high fence that separated his garden from his neighbor's when what should come flying through the air but a particularly beautiful borzoi! One of the more athletic of his neighbor's hounds had managed to clear the fence in one almighty bound, and for a moment Chagall was stupefied—he really thought the dog was airborne, so slow and graceful was its leap.

Inspiration struck, and the artist began to paint flying dogs. Eventually he started to add little houses and fences, and then figures—until there was no room left for dogs, only the magical canvases featuring figures and landscapes that we associate with Chagall today.

What a shame that most of the dog paintings seem to have disappeared. If the one shown here is anything to go by, they would surely have been a howling success.

For several months before American artist Grant Wood completed what is probably one of this century's best-known paintings, he was running short of inspiration. He knew he wanted to pay homage to the spirit of small-town America, its dignity, and Puritanism—but what should he choose as his subject? After much deliberation Wood decided to seek his inspiration in the local architecture—and what should he stumble across but the doghouse pictured here.

The artist was struck by the proud attitude of the kennel's inhabitants, standing guard-like at the threshold of the Gothic arches, and chose to immortalize them. The old pitchfork leaning against the kennel, symbolizing the work ethic of rural America, gave the composition the perfect finishing touch. With his first sketch finished, he rushed home to show the idea to his sister. Only then did he realize that he hadn't asked permission to paint the dogs.

"Don't worry," his sister told him, "the owner's my dentist. I'll introduce you."

Brother and sister took a drive out to visit the dogs' owner that afternoon and were met at the house by a tall gaunt man carrying a pitchfork. Wood grabbed his paints and began working furiously at what he knew deep down was to become an icon of American painting—*American Gothic*. The finished work features as its subjects the artist's sister and the dentist holding the pitchfork. The figures are placed against the backdrop of the dentist's house—of which the kennel was a perfect miniature copy.

This is the extraordinarily sad tale of a dog once owned by the French surrealist painter René Magritte.

For many years the artist kept a very large Great Dane named Bob as his favorite pet. The dog would sit patiently for hours by the studio door absorbed by the creative genius of his master, watching intently as each canvas took shape.

One can imagine Magritte, easel in hand, puffing away on his pipe and occasionally turning to his faithful friend asking, "Well Bob? What do you think?" In response Bob would wag his tail, bark, and pant through a huge grin.

Then one day, sadness came to the studio of René Magritte. A dove landed on the windowsill and began pecking on the glass with its beak. Irritated by the noise, the huge hound got to his feet and raced across the room, launching himself at the dove and unfortunately, the window. The crash was heard streets away, and there are those who still claim to remember watching Bob, with dove in mouth, fly through the air before landing on—and flattening—a passing gentleman in a bowler hat.

Following the funeral, Magritte found it difficult to concentrate and was always turning toward the door, hoping to catch a glimpse of his companion. One day he took a saw and cut out a huge silhouette in exactly the shape and dimensions of Bob—and from then on he was able to work, again although certain motifs associated with that fateful day haunt many of his works.

*E*ver wondered where the expression "let sleeping dogs lie" comes from? This shaggy dog story about the Spanish Surrealist Salvador Dali may well provide a clue.

One evening the filmmaker Luis Buñuel was visiting Dali to discuss their collaboration on the film *Un Chien andalou.* As the night wore on the discussion turned to the topic of man's best friend.

"Of course a dog is a man's best friend," declared Buñuel, citing many instances of canine bravery and loyalty.

"Nonsense" responded Dali. "Sleep is a man's best friend, and quite clearly, a dog's best friend too!" With that, he pointed to his old basset hound who was sprawled, as if melted, across a pile of books, frames, brushes, and assorted debris.

"But it is a fragile friendship, as I shall show you. If any of the underpinning objects are removed, the sleeper will awake." To demonstrate this, the artist removed a single book from beneath his pet's head and, via a series of spasms and stretches, the dog announced its awakening with a big yawn.

The image of fragile sleep so appealed to Dali that he immediately set about exploring the theme on canvas. The painting shown here is a little-known work, believed to have been the first in the famous series.

Francis Bacon's subject matter is often regarded as provocative. His paintings exhibit strange movement and feature ghost-like figures—to many, they just look blurred. But they gained him fame.

So how did this eccentric who, it is reported, would lock himself in his studio from time to time and consume vast quantities of champagne, arrive at this style of painting?

Well, as chance would have it, the painting here recently turned up among some empty wine crates in the artist's cellar. This uncharacteristically "static" painting throws light on a significant period of development in Bacon's style. At the time it was painted, the artist is believed to have been going through a particularly rough patch and had lost all inspiration. Then, out of the blue, a bulldog ambled into his studio. The artist fell in love at first sight with the friendly mutt and named him Bollinger. As eccentric as his new owner, Bollinger's favorite place to sit was right on top of the artist's stylish green record player. He looked so comical in that pose that Bacon painted the scene.

But no sooner had he completed the final brush strokes than a rather devilish plan hatched in the artist's mind. The dog looked so comfortable and contented sitting on the turntable that Bacon felt compelled to switch the record player on just to see the placid fellow's reaction. Well, Bollinger didn't budge an inch. He sat rooted to the spot and spun and spun until he became a blur. Bacon captured what he saw in paint, and his frenetic style was established in an instant. Take a look at *Study of a Dog* to see what became of poor Bollinger.

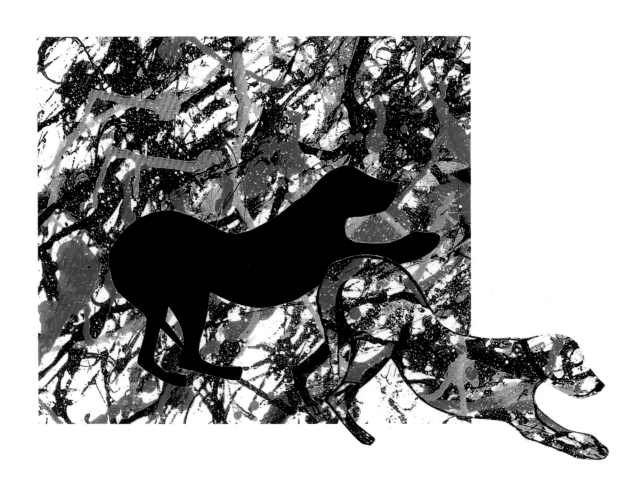

Jackson Pollock is an artist well-known for his exceptional capacity to incorporate paint spills, splashes, or drips into his work.

On one notable occasion, Marcus—Pollock's faithful Labrador—was out roaming when he came across a gang of kids busy scrawling graffiti on the side of a bridge. Seeing the dog, these budding artists decided it would be cool to paint him instead. Marcus thought it was a wonderful game, the paint tickled, and all the attention was great. When completely decorated, he skipped home to the studio, lay down on a big clean white canvas that his master had taken hours preparing, and dozed off.

"Hello boy!" called Pollock as he entered the room. Well, Marcus was so excited and keen to communicate the wonderful adventure that he'd had that he wriggled and twisted on the floor, wagged his tail, sniffed the ground and sneezed... all those exceptional moves that a dog makes when very happy. The result was this wonderful canvas and a source of never-ending inspiration for the artist.

If there is one artist who could be called the Big Daddy of American Pop Art it is Roy Lichtenstein. He was able to capture the aesthetics of America in the 1960s and did more to popularize the comic book aesthetic than anyone else. It thought by some that the early work featured here was the original inspiration for his famous style. It all happened when his writer-friend Brad recounted a story about his little dog, Sally. It was a Sunday evening and Brad had been away all week…

"My dog, a pretty bitch by the name of Sally, had missed me a lot. By the time I got home, she was all over me—panting and licking me. I leaned over, my face close to hers; our eyes locked on each other. I'd talked to her on the phone from Manhattan and promised her everything to stave off the tears. But now I was going to have to let her down. I drew my lips close to her ear and whispered, 'We're gonna have to give Central Park a miss tonight honey…something's come up.' Her gaze widened. She could read the tone in my voice. Her head slid to one side as her heavy lashes flicked unseen tears away and I thought I heard her say… 'But Brad…you promised….'"

Lichtenstein loved the story so much that he immortalized the moment in the shape of a comic strip scene. He would have just left it pinned to the wall had Brad not seen it and flipped. "It's great Roy!" he exclaimed. "Do a series and you're in the big time!" And so the picture remains—and the eyes say it all.

This is the tale of how Andy Warhol's psychedelic prints of a certain famous lady became icons of pop art culture and brought him great fame.

One afternoon during those heady, hippie days, Andy and his friends were chilling out with the help of a pair 3-D glasses that came free with a magazine. It was during this excursion through the blurred pages of nonsense, wearing one red and one green eyepiece, that Andy noticed something colorful move across his studio, crossing from one pool of colored light to the next.

"Hey, look. Am I tripping or is that Marilyn Monroe crawling across the room!" exclaimed the confused artist.

"Don't be crazy man. Like...that's my dog...Trixie," laughed his friend.

Inspiration struck like a thunderbolt, and Warhol disappeared to make multiple screenings in various colors of the image he saw. And yes, it does look like Marilyn Monroe in an odd, doggie sort of way. It was a nice effect, but sadly, it didn't appeal to many people. All that was changed when he decided to feature the *real* Marilyn, and poor old Trixie was robbed of her fifteen minutes of fame.

First published by MQ Publications, Ltd.
254-258 Goswell Road, London EC1V 7RL

Copyright © MQ Publications, Ltd. 1999

Illustrated by Maurice Broughton, with additional material by Vicky Cox
Designed by Alison Shackleton

Illustrations © Maurice Broughton 1999
Text © David Baird 1999

Published in the United States in 1999 by
Stewart, Tabori & Chang
A division of U.S. Media Holdings, Inc.
115 West 18th Street
New York, NY 10011

Distributed in Canada by
General Publishing Company Ltd.
30 Lesmill Road
Don Mills, Ontario, Canada M3B 2T6

Library of Congress Card Catalog Number: 99-63653

ISBN 1-55670-932-3
Printed in Italy

10 9 8 7 6 5 4 3 2 1

First Printing